British Citizenship Test

Practice Questions

Questions and answers for the Life in the UK Test

Published by Red Squirrel Publishing

Red Squirrel Publishing
Suite 235, 77 Beak Street,
London, W1F 9DB, United Kingdom

sales@redsquirrelbooks.com
www.redsquirrelbooks.com

First Edition - First Impression

Although the authors and publisher have
made every effort to ensure the accuracy and
completeness of information contained in this book,
we assume no responsibility for errors, inaccuracies,
omissions or any inconsistency herein.

ISBN-10: 0-9552159-0-0
ISBN-13: 978-0-9552159-0-2

Edited by Henry Dillon and Alastair Smith
Designed and artworked by Cox Design Partnership,
Witney, Oxon
Printed and bound in the United Kingdom

CONTENTS

INTRODUCTION

Welcome to the **British Citizenship Test: Practice Questions** exercise book. This book has been designed to test your knowledge of the official study materials before sitting the *Life in the UK Test*. Please take some time to read through this section carefully. It tells you about all the features of this book and will enable you to get as much out of it as possible.

How to prepare for the Test

The *Life in the UK Test* is based on official study materials provided by the Home Office. These have been published in a handbook called *Life in the United Kingdom: A Journey to Citizenship* and can also be found in our companion *British Citizenship Test: Study Guide*. Further details about the study guide can be found in the back of this book.

Before you start your revision, note that you will only be tested on Chapters 2, 3 and 4 of the study materials. The questions in this book will only test these chapters.

Once you've completed studying the study materials thoroughly you should check you are ready to take the test by completing several practice tests from this book. You should complete each 24 question practice test within 45 minutes and aim for a pass rate of at least 75% – or only six incorrect answers.

If you do not pass the practice tests satisfactorily or do not feel confident enough to sit the test then you should continue your revision. If you do not have sufficient revision time left, then you may be able to reschedule your test appointment. Most test centres are happy to do this if you give them reasonable notice. Contact your test centre for more details.

How to use this exercise book

The practice tests in this book closely match the format and content of the official test.

There are nine practice tests in this book. Each practice test is made up of 24 questions. This is exactly the same format as the official test. Each of the practice tests is different and will contain questions covering all parts of the study materials.

To make scoring easier, cut out the marking sheet at the back of this book and use this to record your answers. The answers for each test are provided in the back of the book.

Check our website www.redsquirrelbooks.com for the latest updates to this book and for extra study tips.

If you have any thoughts on how we can improve this publication then we'd be very keen to hear from you. You can email your thoughts to us at feedback@redsquirrelbooks.com

Good luck with your test.

PRACTICE TEST 1

1 **The UK restricted its immigration laws in the 1970s – however which two locations did Britain admit refugees from during this time?**

    A Ethiopia

    B South East Asia

    C Turkey

    D Uganda

2 **How long was Britain at war during the Second World War?**

    A 2 years

    B 4 years

    C 6 years

    D 8 years

3 **At what ages do school children take compulsory tests?**

    A 5, 10 and 15

    B 6, 10 and 14

    C 7, 11 and 14

    D 8, 12 and 15

4 **What percentage of the workforce are women?**

    A 40%

    B 45%

    C 51%

    D 65%

5   What was the population of the United Kingdom in 2001?

    A   38.3 million

    B   48.1 million

    C   58.8 million

    D   98.3 million

6   How often is a census carried out in the United Kingdom?

    A   Once every five years

    B   Once every eight years

    C   Once every ten years

    D   Whenever the government decides

7   According to the 2001 Census, what percentage of the UK population reported that they had a religion?

    A   35%

    B   55%

    C   65%

    D   75%

8   What is the distance from the north coast of Scotland to the south coast of England?

    A   Approximately 500 kilometres

    B   Approximately 1,000 kilometres

    C   Approximately 2,000 kilometres

    D   Approximately 10,000 kilometres

9 What is the Grand National?

    A A major UK high street bank

    B A popular horse racing event

    C A train connecting London and Cardiff

    D The name of the national lottery

10 What is traditionally eaten on Christmas Day?

    A Beer-battered cod and chips

    B Poached salmon and rice pudding

    C Roast pork and trifle

    D Roast turkey and Christmas Pudding

11 What does Remembrance Day commemorate?

    A The appreciation of single mothers

    B The celebration of community

    C The crucifixion of Jesus Christ

    D The memory of those who died during war

12 What tradition is observed in the period before Remembrance Day?

    A People dress in black

    B People eat Remembrance Cakes

    C People give flowers to community elders

    D People wear artificial poppies in buttonholes

13 When is the national day for Wales?

    A 1 March

    B 17 March

    C 23 April

    D 30 November

14 Where are government statements usually reported as coming from?

    A Buckingham Palace

    B Number Ten

    C Stormont

    D Clarence House

15 What happens during Question Time?

    A Government Ministers present new policies for debate

    B Members of Parliament may ask questions of Government Ministers

    C Members of Parliament take questions from the press

    D Members of the public can ask questions of their local MP

16 Which of the following statements is not true about the constitutional role of the monarch? Select two options from below

    A They must always follow the Prime Minister's advice

    B They may express their political opinions in public

    C They should criticise government policy if they do not believe it serves the public interest

    D They are responsible for opening and closing parliament

17 Where is the House of Commons?

    A In Buckingham Palace

    B In the Palace of Westminster

    C In Windsor Castle

    D In Clarence House

18 **What is the name of the system that governs how MPs are elected into the House of Commons?**

    A Aggregated vote system

    B Electoral college system

    C First past the post system

    D Proportional representation system

19 **What is a Civil Servant?**

    A Any person who has a job carrying out government policy

    B Any person who is a member of a political party

    C Any person who is a Member of Parliament

    D Any person who works for a member of the House of Lords

20 **The Scottish Parliament has powers to vary national income tax. Is this statement true or false?**

    A True

    B False

21 **When was the second referendum for a Scottish Parliament?**

    A 1962

    B 1979

    C 1987

    D 1997

22 **What is the population of all countries that are part of the Commonwealth?**

    A 500 million people

    B 900 million people

    C 1.7 billion people

    D 3.5 billion people

23 **What were the terms of the first agreement that European countries committed to, which led to the forming of the European Union?**

   A   To allow free and unrestricted travel for citizens of all member states

   B   To agree to adopt a single currency

   C   To form a single European parliament that would shape common European legislation

   D   To put all their coal and steel production under the control of a single authority

24 **Which of the following statements about the European Parliament is not correct?**

   A   It debates and scrutinises decisions of the European Commission

   B   It decides EU policy

   C   It has the power to refuse to agree EU expenditure

   D   It is based in Strasbourg

PRACTICE TEST 2

1 **During 1948, what were immigrants from Ireland and the West Indies invited into the UK to do?**

    A Work in textile mills

    B Aid the reconstruction effort after the Second World War

    C Drive buses and taxis in local towns and villages

    D Help build canals and railways

2 **Since 1951, the UK population has grown faster than the average growth for countries in the European Union. Is this statement true or false?**

    A True

    B False

3 **What percentage of children live with both birth parents?**

    A 45%

    B 50%

    C 65%

    D 80%

4 **When did married women gain the right to retain ownership of their own money and property?**

    A 1752

    B 1792

    C 1810

    D 1882

5   What is the population of Northern Ireland?

    A 0.9 million

    B 1.7 million

    C 2.5 million

    D 3.1 million

6   How many years must have passed before an individual's census form is viewable by the public?

    A 10 years

    B 50 years

    C 100 years

    D An individual's census form is confidential and never viewable by the public

7   Which other name can be used to refer to the Church of England?

    A The Anglican Church

    B The Catholic Church

    C The Methodist Church

    D The Presbyterian Church

8   What is the distance of the widest part across England and Wales?

    A Approximately 500 kilometres

    B Approximately 1,000 kilometres

    C Approximately 2,000 kilometres

    D Approximately 10,000 kilometres

9   What does the British abbreviation FA stand for?

    A   A Federal Agent

    B   The Football Association

    C   The Fourth Amendment

    D   The Fine Arts

10   Where is it believed that Father Christmas folklore originated?

    A   From Dutch, German and Swedish settlers emigrating to America

    B   From early Catholic beliefs

    C   From Russian tsars wanting to encourage gift giving

    D   From Christmas advertising campaigns for a major soft drink company

11   What traditionally happens on St Valentine's Day?

    A   Couples fast from eating

    B   Couples visit the elderly together

    C   Couples play tricks on each other

    D   Couples send cards to each other

12   When did the First World War end?

    A   28 February 1914

    B   11 November 1918

    C   21 November 1925

    D   8 May 1945

13 What is the name of the ministerial position that is responsible for foreign affairs?

    A Chancellor of the Exchequer

    B Foreign Secretary

    C Home Secretary

    D Lord Chancellor

14 How many politicians are there in the Cabinet?

    A About 10

    B About 20

    C About 30

    D About 40

15 When are by-elections held?

    A Every six months

    B Every two years

    C Every three years

    D Only when an MP resigns or dies while in office

16 The monarch can reject laws and decisions made by government and the Cabinet. Is this statement true or false?

    A True

    B False

17 How many constituencies are there throughout the United Kingdom?

    A 350

    B 645

    C 750

    D 1,000

18 What must a candidate achieve in order to win their constituency?

    A Be a member of the party that wins government office

    B Win at least 25% of the votes within their constituency

    C Win at least 15,000 votes

    D Win the most votes out of all candidates in their constituency

19 Which one of the following parliaments or assemblies does not use proportional representation?

    A Scottish Parliament

    B Welsh Assembly

    C Northern Ireland Assembly

    D House of Commons

20 What are the two key features of the civil service? Select two options from below

    A Business knowledge

    B Neutrality

    C Party loyalty

    D Professionalism

21 How many Members of the Scottish Parliament (MSPs) are there?

    A 97

    B 158

    C 129

    D 105

22 Which of the following statements about the Good Friday Agreement is not correct?

    A It was created in 1982

    B It was endorsed by the Irish and British governments

    C It was signed by the IRA and the UDA

    D The Northern Ireland Assembly was established shortly afterwards

23 How many member states are there in the Commonwealth?

    A 25 member states

    B 39 member states

    C 54 member states

    D 75 member states

24 When did Britain join the European Economic Community?

    A 1935

    B 1959

    C 1973

    D 1992

PRACTICE TEST 3

1   During the 1950s, textile and engineering firms from the UK sent recruitment agents to which two countries? Select two countries from below

    A India

    B Pakistan

    C Poland

    D South Africa

2   What work did migrant Irish labourers do in the UK during the Irish famine?

    A Construct canals and railways

    B Drive local buses

    C Teach in schools

    D Work in textile mills

3   What proportion of women with children (of school age) also work?

    A One quarter

    B Half

    C Two thirds

    D Three quarters

4   Very few people believe that women in Britain should stay at home and not go out to paid work. Is this statement true or false?

    A True

    B False

5   How much has the UK population grown by (in percentage terms) since 1951?

    A 5%

    B 17%

    C 23%

    D 34%

6   What percentage of the United Kingdom's population is made up of ethnic minorities?

    A 1.3%

    B 7.9%

    C 10.8%

    D 22.3%

7   What is the title of the King or Queen within the Church of England?

    A Archbishop of Canterbury

    B Governor General

    C Head Priest

    D Supreme Governor

8   What are the two most widespread Christian denominations in Wales? Select two options from below

    A Baptist

    B Catholic

    C Methodist

    D Presbyterian

9 Where is the popular UK tennis tournament played in South London?

    A Putney

    B Richmond

    C Twickenham

    D Wimbledon

10 What does Boxing Day celebrate?

    A Appreciation of gifts received on Christmas Day

    B Appreciation of work by servants and trades people

    C Recycling the packaging used to pack Christmas gifts

    D The British Heavyweight Boxing Championship

11 When is Mothering Sunday?

    A One week before Easter

    B Two weeks before Easter

    C Three weeks before Easter

    D Four weeks before Easter

12 When is Remembrance Day?

    A 1 May

    B 31 August

    C 21 October

    D 11 November

13 What happens to policy & law decisions once they have been agreed by Cabinet?

    A They are published in the local newspapers for public debate

    B They are signed by the Prime Minister making them law

    C They are submitted to Parliament for approval

    D They are submitted to the King or Queen for royal assent

14 How often does the Cabinet normally meet?

    A Daily

    B Weekly

    C Bi-weekly

    D Monthly

15 Newspapers can not publish political opinions or run campaigns to influence government. Is this statement true or false?

    A True

    B False

16 During a general election, the main parties are given free time on radio and television to make short party political broadcasts. Is this statement true or false?

    A True

    B False

17 How is the Speaker of the House of Commons chosen?

    A Appointed by the King or Queen

    B Chosen by the Prime Minister

    C Elected by fellow MPs

    D Elected by the public

18 **Where is proportional representation not used in UK politics?**

    A House of Commons

    B Northern Ireland Assembly

    C Scottish Parliament

    D Welsh Assembly

19 **Which of the following statements about non-departmental public bodies is not correct?**

    A Parliament can abolish or change their powers and roles

    B They may propose new laws to the House of Commons

    C They are semi-independent agencies set up by the government

    D They are sometimes called quangos

20 **Which of the following parliaments or assemblies use proportional representation?**

    A European Parliament

    B Northern Ireland Assembly

    C Scottish Parliament

    D All of the above

21 **When was the civil service reformed to prevent corruption and favouritism?**

    A Early 15th century

    B Early 17th century

    C Early 18th century

    D Early 19th century

22 What can the Scottish Parliament do that the Welsh Assembly can not? Select two options from below

A Appoint Members of Scottish Parliament to the House of Lords

B Debate laws governing defence, foreign affairs and social security

C Make changes in the lower base rate of income tax

D Pass legislation on anything not specifically reserved for Westminster

23 What is the purpose of the United Nations?

A To prevent war and maintain peace and security

B To create a single market for all world nations

C To create global laws to regulate foreign affairs

D To debate global third world development and funding proposals

24 What is the main aim behind the European Union today?

A For member states to observe a single set of laws

B For member states to improve efficiency

C For member states to protect human rights in Europe

D For member states to become a single market

PRACTICE TEST 4

1 Name three countries that Jewish people migrated from (and into the UK) to escape persecution during 1880–1910

    A France, Germany, Poland

    B Germany, Austria, Italy

    C Poland, Ukraine, Belarus

    D Portugal, Spain, Ukraine

2 What is the percentage difference in pay between male and female hourly pay rates?

    A Women receive 5% lower pay than men

    B Women receive 10% lower pay than men

    C Women receive 20% lower pay than men

    D No difference – women are paid the same as men

3 When do young people take GCSE examinations?

    A 15 years old

    B 16 years old

    C 17 years old

    D 18 years old

4 What is the population of England?

    A 23.4 million

    B 38.1 million

    C 49.1 million

    D 58.8 million

5   What is the largest ethnic minority in Britain?

    A Bangladeshi descent

    B Black Caribbean descent

    C Indian descent

    D Pakistani descent

6   What year did the Church of England come in to existence?

    A 1444

    B 1534

    C 1644

    D 1754

7   Where is the Welsh language widely spoken?

    A Highlands and Islands of Scotland

    B Ireland

    C Southern England

    D Wales

8   Which of the UK national days is celebrated with a public holiday?

    A St Andrew's Day in Scotland

    B St David's Day in Wales

    C St George's Day in England

    D St Patrick's Day in Northern Ireland (and the Republic of Ireland)

9   When is New Year celebrated in the United Kingdom?

    A 25 December

    B 31 December

    C 1 January

    D 1 March

10   What traditionally happens on Mothering Sunday?

   A Mothers make special meals for their family

   B People hold fireworks displays

   C People celebrate the mother of Jesus Christ

   D People give gifts to their mothers

11   The UK birth rate was at an all time high in 2002. Is this statement true or false?

   A True

   B False

12   What is the abbreviation MP short for?

   A Master of Parliament

   B Member of Parliament

   C Member of Party

   D Minister of Parliament

13   What is the name of the ministerial position that is responsible for the economy?

   A Chancellor of the Exchequer

   B Chief Whip

   C Home Secretary

   D Lord Chancellor

14   What is the name of the official record of proceedings in Parliament?

   A Hansard

   B Parliament News

   C The Recorder

   D Westminster Hour

15 Which of the following statements is correct about political reporting in the UK? Select two options from below

   A All reporting on radio and television must be balanced

   B Politicians must be able to read interview questions beforehand

   C Newspapers usually have their own angle in reporting political events

   D It is illegal for newspapers to run campaigns to influence government policy

16 What are the roles of the Whips in parliament? Select two correct roles from below

   A Ensure discipline and attendance of MPs at voting time in the House of Commons

   B Ensure the House of Commons is always safe and secure

   C Keep order in the House of Commons during political debates

   D Negotiate with the Speaker over the parliamentary timetable and order of business

17 Judges are independent of the Crown. Is this statement true or false?

   A True

   B False

18 Which of the following would not be considered part of a lobby group?

   A Commercial organisations

   B Industrial organisations

   C Ordinary citizens

   D Professional organisations

19 Where do local authority services get most of their funding from?

A Central government taxation

B Lottery grants

C Issuing parking tickets

D Local council tax

20 What is the Northern Ireland Parliament often called?

A Belfast

B Westminster

C Stormont

D UDA

21 What is Britain's role within the United Nations?

A Member of the UN Security Council

B Provides a neutral location for hosting UN meetings in Scotland

C Selects the UN Secretary General from members of the Security Council

D All of the above

22 Which country does not have its own parliament or national assembly?

A England

B Northern Ireland

C Scotland

D Wales

23 **Which of the following statements about the Commonwealth is not correct?**

    A It has a common language

    B It has a membership of 54 states

    C It has 10% of the world's population

    D The Crown is the symbolic head

24 **Which of these statements is correct?**

    A Citizens of the European Union must have a valid work permit to work in any EU member state

    B Citizens of the European Union have the right to work in any EU member state

PRACTICE TEST 5

1   During the 1950s, Britain set up bus driver recruitment centres in which location?

   A   Australia

   B   Ireland

   C   Canada

   D   West Indies

2   Which countries were invited to provide immigrant workers to help British reconstruction after the Second World War?

   A   Canada and France

   B   Germany and Holland

   C   Ireland and the West Indies

   D   Poland and Ukraine

3   How often do most children in the UK receive their pocket money?

   A   Every day

   B   Every month

   C   Every week

   D   Only on their birthday

4   When do young people take A/S and A level examinations?

   A   14 and 15 years old

   B   15 and 16 years old

   C   16 and 17 years old

   D   17 and 18 years old

5   What is the population of Wales?

    A   1.2 million

    B   2.9 million

    C   3.4 million

    D   5.3 million

6   What overall proportion of Britain's African Caribbean, Pakistani, Indian and Bangladeshi communities were born in Britain?

    A   About one quarter

    B   About one third

    C   About half

    D   About three quarters

7   According to the Church of England, heirs to the throne are not allowed to marry who?

    A   Anyone who is not of royal blood

    B   Anyone who is not Protestant

    C   Anyone who is under the age of 25

    D   Anyone who was born outside the UK

8   Where is the Gaelic language spoken?

    A   Highlands and Islands of Scotland

    B   Cornwall

    C   Southern England

    D   Wales

9 **How many bank holidays are there each year in the United Kingdom?**

    A Two

    B Four

    C Nine

    D Ten

10 **According to tradition if you were the first visitor of the new year to a Scottish home, what might you be expected to bring?**

    A A bag of ice and whisky

    B A block of butter and whisky

    C Coal, bread and whisky

    D Milk, tartan cloth and whisky

11 **When is April Fool's Day?**

    A 1 February

    B 1 March

    C 1 April

    D 1 May

12 **How often are general elections held in the UK?**

    A At least once every two years

    B At least once every three years

    C At least once every five years

    D At least once every six years

13 What is the role of the Cabinet?

   A To decide general policies for government

   B To examine laws proposed by the House of Commons

   C To investigate serious complaints against the police

   D To provide royal assent for new laws

14 How are Whips appointed?

   A By their party leaders

   B By the King or Queen

   C By the Prime Minister

   D By vote amongst their peers

15 Where does the monarch deliver their speech from at the start of a new parliamentary session?

   A From a throne in Buckingham Palace

   B From a throne in the House of Lords

   C From a throne in the House of Commons

   D From a throne in Windsor Castle

16 What famous phrase describes the level of expression that the monarch is restricted to when discussing government matters?

   A Advise, warn and encourage

   B Advocate, promote and support

   C Direct, track and monitor

   D Discuss, debate and review

17 In the past, what were the only two ways that members could be appointed to the House of Lords? Select two answers from below

   A By being hereditary aristocrats

   B By being rewarded with peerage for their public service

   C By being voted into the House of Lords by public election

   D By serving at least twenty years as an MP in the House of Commons

18 Can a judge challenge the legality of a law?

   A Yes, but only if they do not believe the law is fair

   B Yes, but only if the law would contravene human rights

   C Yes, but they must seek the Prime Minister's approval first

   D No, they must apply the law as agreed by the House of Commons

19 When are local government elections held?

   A April every two years

   B June and December each year

   C May each year

   D September each year

20 How are new judges selected?

   A All lawyers with over twenty years experience may enter a lottery ballot

   B By a special parliamentary committee

   C From nominations put forward by existing judges

   D The King or Queen takes advice from the Prime Minister

21 When was the Northern Ireland Parliament established?

  A 1922

  B 1938

  C 1945

  D 1956

22 What is the role of the Council of Ministers?

  A Debate proposals, decisions and expenditure
     of the European Commission

  B Judge and give verdicts on European court
     cases that have been appealed

  C Ensure EU regulations and directives are being
     followed by other member states

  D Propose new laws and decisions regarding the EU

**23 Britain has an aging population and has a record number of
people aged 85 and over. Is this statement true or false?**

  A True

  B False

24 What is the current voting age?

  A 16 years old

  B 18 years old

  C 20 years old

  D 21 years old

PRACTICE TEST 6

1 **Why did Irish migrants come to Britain during the mid 1840s?**

    A To escape famine

    B To escape religious persecution

    C To invade and seize land

    D To seek refuge from war

2 **When did women get voting rights at the same age as men?**

    A 1840

    B 1918

    C 1928

    D 1945

3 **How many young people (up to the age of 19) are there in the UK?**

    A 5 million

    B 10 million

    C 15 million

    D 20 million

4 **What is the minimum age for buying alcohol?**

    A 14

    B 16

    C 18

    D 21

5 What is the population of Scotland?

 A 1.3 million

 B 3.2 million

 ❋ **C** 5.1 million

 D 7.8 million

6 What percentage of London's residents are ethnic minorities?

 A 12%

 ❋ **B** 29%

 C 40%

 D 55%

7 What must a monarch swear to do as part of their coronation?

 A To advise the Prime Minister on state affairs

 B To appoint their heir to the throne

 C To maintain the protestant religion in the United Kingdom

 D To reign as monarch for at least 20 years

8 When is Christmas celebrated?

 A 25 November

 B 24 December

 ❋ **C** 25 December

 D 1 January

9 **If you were visiting a Welsh home at New Year, what tradition might be observed?**

A A new doormat is placed at the front door to welcome visitors into the new year

B The back door is opened to release the old year, then shut and locked, and then the front door opened to let in the new year

C All of the windows of the house are opened for an hour to release the old year

D All of the above

10 **What traditionally happens on April Fool's day?**

A It is a public holiday until noon

B People play jokes on each other

C People enjoy public firework displays

D None of the above

11 **What is the role of the Prime Minister? Select two options from below**

A Appoints ministers of state and other public positions

B Leader of the party in power

C Make new laws effective by signing legislation

D Perform the duties of Head of State

12 **How is it decided which party forms the Government?**

A The members of the House of Lords vote for their preferred party

B The party with the most candidates forms the Government

C The party with the most MPs elected into the House of Commons forms the Government

D The party with the most votes forms the Government

13 What percentage of the UK population is made up of ethnic minorities?

A About 2%

B About 8%

C About 15%

D About 25%

14 Who is the current heir to the throne?

A The Duke of Edinburgh

B The Duke of York

C Prince William

D The Prince of Wales

15 In what year did the Prime Minister gain powers to be able to appoint members of the House of Lords?

A 1957

B 1968

C 1973

D 1980

16 Who of the following are automatically members of the House of Lords? Choose two answers from below

A Mayors from local government

B Most senior judges

C Senior Bishops of the Church of England

D MPs who are also members of the Cabinet

17 Who appoints new judges?

    A Chief Justice

    B Home Secretary

    C King or Queen

    D Lord Chancellor

18 In which year were the Assembly for Wales and the Scottish Parliament created?

    A 1969

    B 1972

    C 1982

    D 1999

19 When did the government start a programme of devolved administration for Wales and Scotland?

    A 1979

    B 1982

    C 1997

    D 2001

20 When was the Good Friday Agreement signed?

    A 1945

    B 1956

    C 1973

    D 1998

21 Where is the European Commission based?

    A Paris

    B Geneva

    C Strasbourg

    D Brussels

22 From the list below, which is not a right or duty of UK citizens?

    A Right to vote in all elections

    B Duty to perform jury service

    C Duty to perform military service

    D Right to welfare benefits

23 When was the current voting age set?

    A 1945

    B 1956

    C 1969

    D 1982

24 Which of the following statements about the electoral register is not correct?

    A British citizens have the right to have their name placed on the electoral register

    B Local authorities must make the electoral register available for anyone to view

    C The register is held at local electoral registration offices

    D You must be at least 21 years old to have your name on the register

PRACTICE TEST 7

1 **Why did large numbers of Jewish people come to Britain during 1880–1910?**

    A To escape famine

    B To escape the violence they faced at home

    C To invade and seize land

    D None of the above

2 **What year did women in the UK gain the right to divorce their husband?**

    A 1810

    B 1857

    C 1901

    D 1945

3 **What proportion of young people enrol to go on to higher education after school?**

    A One in two

    B One in three

    C One in four

    D All young people move on to higher education

4 **What is the minimum age for buying tobacco?**

    A 14

    B 16

    C 18

    D 21

BRITISH CITIZENSHIP TEST: PRACTICE QUESTIONS

5   In which year will the next UK census be carried out?

    A   2008

    B   2011

    C   2015

    D   2020

6   What percentage of UK's ethnic minorities live in the London area?

    A   14%

    B   30%

    C   45%

    D   60%

7   Who ceremonially appoints a new Archbishop of Canterbury?

    A   The exiting Archbishop of Canterbury

    B   The Home Secretary

    C   The King or Queen

    D   The Prime Minister

8   Where is the Geordie dialect spoken?

    A   Cornwall

    B   Liverpool

    C   London

    D   Tyneside

9   What does Christmas day celebrate?

    A   The birth of Jesus Christ

    B   The death of Jesus Christ

    C   The miracles of Jesus Christ

    D   The resurrection of Jesus Christ

10 When is Easter celebrated?

A   In December or January each year

B   In June or July each year

C   In March or April each year

D   In May or June each year

11 What does Guy Fawkes Night commemorate?

A   Remembrance of those killed during war

B   The Gunpowder Plot of 1605

C   The invention of fireworks

D   The rebuilding of the Houses of Parliament

12 What did the Prime Minister used to be called in Latin?

A   Primus dominis

B   Primus inter pares

C   Primus obter dictum

D   Primus ad mortem

13 What percentage of the UK's population live in England?

A   53%

B   68%

C   75%

D   83%

14 What type of constitution does the UK have?

A   A legal constitution

B   A written constitution

C   An amended constitution

D   An unwritten constitution

15 In which year did Queen Elizabeth II start her reign?

    A   1945

    B   1952

    C   1963

    D   1972

16 What is a Life Peer?

    A   A hereditary aristocrat or peer of the realm

    B   A member of the House of Lords who has been appointed by the Prime Minister

    C   Any person who has inherited a peerage from their family

    D   Any person who has served as a MP for more than twenty years

17 What is the name of the largest police force in the United Kingdom?

    A   Humberside

    B   Merseyside

    C   The Bill

    D   The Metropolitan Police

18 Who is responsible for investigating serious complaints against the police?

    A   The Lord Chancellor

    B   The Home Secretary

    C   The Chief of Police

    D   An independent authority

19 Where is the National Assembly for Wales situated?

A Cardiff

B Edinburgh

C Stormont

D Swansea

20 How many members are there in the Northern Ireland Assembly?

A 64 members

B 82 members

C 108 members

D 125 members

21 What is the role of the European Parliament?

A Propose new laws and make decisions regarding the EU

B Ensure EU regulations and directives are being followed by member states

C Judge and give verdicts on European court cases that have been appealed

D To scrutinise and debate the proposals, decisions and expenditure of the European Commission

22 The Council of Europe has no power to make laws. Is this statement true or false?

A True

B False

23 What is the minimum age for standing for public office?

A 18 years

B 21 years

C 25 years

D 30 years

24 Citizens from which of the following countries are not eligible to stand for office in the UK?

A Citizens from Commonwealth countries

B European citizens

C Irish Republic citizens

D United Kingdom citizens

PRACTICE TEST 8

1   Why did Protestant Huguenots from France come to Britain?

   A   To escape famine

   B   To escape religious persecution

   C   To invade and seize land

   D   To seek refuge from war

2   When did women first get the right to vote?

   A   1840

   B   1901

   C   1918

   D   1945

3   How many children (under 18) are estimated to be working in the United Kingdom at any time?

   A   One million

   B   Two million

   C   Five million

   D   Eight million

4   Why was a census not carried out in the United Kingdom in 1941?

   A   Because Britain was at war

   B   Because it was abolished by the government

   C   Because it was boycotted by the public

   D   No census was planned for that year

5 According to the 2001 Census, what percentage of people stated their religion as Muslim?

A 1%

B 3%

C 15%

D 21%

6 What is the Church of Scotland also known as?

A The Kirk

B The Murray

C The Stormont

D The Westminster

7 Where is the Scouse dialect spoken?

A Cornwall

B Liverpool

C London

D Tyneside

8 According to tradition, when are Christmas presents opened?

A On Boxing Day

B On Christmas Day

C On Christmas Eve

D On New Year's Eve

9   What do Easter eggs symbolise?

A   Fertility and progress

B   Good health and proper eating

C   New life and the coming of spring

D   Youth and happiness

10   When is Guy Fawkes Night?

A   The evening of 15 October

B   The evening of 25 September

C   The evening of 30 May

D   The evening of 5 November

11   What is the name of the ministerial position that is responsible for order and immigration?

A   Chancellor of the Exchequer

B   Chief Whip

C   Home Secretary

D   Lord Chancellor

12   What percentage of London's population is made up of ethnic minorities?

A   9% of London's population

B   15% of London's population

C   29% of London's population

D   45% of London's population

13 What is the second largest party in the House of Commons called by convention?

A Her Majesty's Loyal Opposition

B Shadow Cabinet

C The Conservation Party

D The Labour Party

14 Which politicians are members of the Shadow Cabinet?

A The remaining MPs in Government who are not in the Cabinet

B Peers from the House of Lords

C Civil servants working for the government

D Senior members of the main opposition party

15 Select the two correct ceremonial duties that the King or Queen performs from the options below

A Chairing proceedings in the House of Lords

B Debating political opinions with the Prime Minister

C Opening and closing of parliament

D Reading the "Queen's (or King's) Speech"

16 What are the two main roles of the House of Lords? Select two options from below

A To create and shape new laws

B To examine laws proposed by the House of Commons in detail and at greater leisure

C To represent everyone in each member's constituency

D To suggest amendments or changes to laws proposed by the House of Commons

17 Where are the headquarters of the Metropolitan Police force?

A 20 Downing Street

B London Bridge

C New Scotland Yard

D Tower of London

18 Which of the following is not a service provided by local authorities?

A Education

B Refuse collection

C Fire service

D None – they are all services provided by local authorities

19 How many Assembly Members are there in the National Assembly for Wales?

A About 30 members

B About 40 members

C About 50 members

D About 60 members

20 What is the purpose of the Council of Europe?

A To create a single market for participating members of the council

B To debate proposals, decisions and expenditure of the European Commission

C To protect human rights and seek solutions to problems facing European society

D To create new European regulations and directives

21 **Which two statements form the true definition of an EU regulation? Select two options from below**

A EU Regulations must be adopted and implemented by each EU member state by a set time

B EU Regulations automatically have force in all EU member states

C EU Regulations can not override national legislation

D EU Regulations override national legislation

22 **The Council of Ministers has no power to propose new laws. Is this statement true or false?**

A True

B False

23 **How do you register to vote?**

A Complete an electoral registration form

B Do nothing – all eligible citizens are automatically registered

C Bring your passport to any polling booth on election day

D Contact your local MP's office

24 **What must a candidate have in order to become a local councillor?**

A A connection with the area in which they wish to take office

B A deposit of £500

C A recommendation from their local MP

D Membership of a political party

PRACTICE TEST 9

1   During the 1980s, the seven largest immigrant groups to the UK were from the United States, Australia, South Africa, New Zealand, Hong Kong, Singapore and Malaysia. Is this statement true or false?

   A   True

   B   False

2   There are more men in study at university than women. Is this statement true or false?

   A   True

   B   False

3   In the 2001 general election, what proportion of first time voters actually cast their vote?

   A   One in two

   B   One in three

   C   One in five

   D   One in eight

4   When was the first census carried out in the United Kingdom?

   A   1785

   B   1801

   C   1851

   D   1912

5 **According to the 2001 Census, what percentage of people who had a religion stated that it was Christian?**

    A   20%

    B   50%

    C   70%

    D   90%

6 **What percentage of the British population are Roman Catholic?**

    A   10%

    B   20%

    C   30%

    D   40%

7 **How does the King or Queen select the Archbishop of Canterbury?**

    A   Based on a public ballot

    B   Based on their own judgement as to who would make a good Archbishop

    C   Using advice from other bishops

    D   Using advice from the Prime Minister who takes a recommendation from a Church appointed committee

8 **Where is the Cockney dialect spoken?**

    A   Cornwall

    B   Liverpool

    C   London

    D   Tyneside

9   What is mistletoe traditionally used for during Christmas?

A   Burned in the fireplace as an aromatic fuel

B   Given to friends and relatives as a symbol of Christmas generosity

C   Hung above doorways under which couples are expected to kiss

D   Used as a spice to make Christmas Pudding

10   What does Easter commemorate?

A   The appointment of a new Archbishop

B   The birth of Jesus Christ

C   The creation of the Church of England

D   The resurrection of Jesus Christ

11   When is St Valentine's Day?

A   1 February

B   14 February

C   1 April

D   14 April

12   Where is the Prime Minister's official residence?

A   10 Downing Street

B   12 Downing Street

C   Buckingham Palace

D   Westminster Palace

13 What is the role of the Speaker in the House of Commons?

A To chair proceedings in the House of Commons

B To ensure discipline and attendance of MPs at voting time in the House of Commons

C To promote Members from the House of Commons to the House of Lords

D To sign new laws agreed in the House of Commons

14 Who is the Head of State of the United Kingdom?

A The Home Secretary

B The King or Queen

C The Prime Minister

D The Speaker of the House of Commons

15 It is possible for a candidate to win a constituency even if they don't win more than half of the votes cast. Is this statement true or false?

A False

B True

16 What other regional language, in addition to English, is also spoken in Scotland?

A French

B Welsh

C Gaelic

D Scottish

17 Who from the list below is not responsible for controlling the administration of the Police?

A   Chief of Police

B   Elected local councillors

C   Home Secretary

D   Magistrates

18 Which of the following statements is not true about British politics?

A   Political party membership in Britain has been declining over the last few years

B   Main political parties have membership branches in every constituency

C   There are no independent MPs in parliament

D   Public opinion polls are very important to the leadership of political parties

19 All candidates standing for office in local government must be members of a political party. Is this statement true or false?

A   True

B   False

20 When was the first referendum for a Scottish Parliament?

A   1962

B   1979

C   1987

D   1997

21 When was the Council of Europe established?

    A 1964

    B 1982

    C 1901

    D 1949

22 Which of the following statements about EU Directives is correct?

    A EU Directives are voluntary and do not have to be observed by EU member states

    B EU Directives automatically have force in all EU member states

    C EU Directives must be introduced and observed within EU member states within a specific time frame

    D EU Directives override national legislation

23 How often are elections held for Members of the European Parliament?

    A Every two years

    B Every three years

    C Every four years

    D Every five years

24 Which of the following is not a requirement for MPs, MEPs or MSPs wishing to stand for office?

    A A local connection within the area in which they wish to take office

    B Citizenship of the United Kingdom, the Irish Republic or the Commonwealth

    C Be over the age of 21 years old

    D Be willing and able to pay a deposit to support their campaign

MARKING SHEET

	Test 1	Test 2	Test 3	Test 4	Test 5	Test 6	Test 7	Test 8	Test 9
1									
2									
3									
4									
5									
6									
7									
8									
9									
10									
11									
12									
13									
14									
15									
16									
17									
18									
19									
20									
21									
22									
23									
24									
Total									

SCORING GUIDE

Check your test results using this scoring guide.

Total correct answers	Grade
Less than 6	Very poor – Do not take any further practice tests until significant revision has been completed.
7–12	Unsatisfactory – Considerable gaps in knowledge. Further revision of study materials required.
13–17	Good – Not quite ready yet. Revise your weak areas to complete your knowledge.
18 or more	Excellent – Well done! You are above the pass mark and are now ready to sit the official test.

ANSWERS

	Test 1	Test 2	Test 3	Test 4	Test 5	Test 6	Test 7	Test 8	Test 9
1	B & D	B	A & B	C	D	A	B	B	A
2	C	B	A	C	C	C	B	C	B
3	C	C	D	B	C	C	B	B	C
4	B	D	A	C	D	C	B	A	B
5	C	B	B	C	B	C	B	B	C
6	C	C	B	B	C	B	C	A	A
7	D	A	D	D	B	C	C	B	D
8	B	A	A & C	D	A	C	D	B	C
9	B	B	D	C	B	B	A	C	C
10	D	A	B	D	C	B	C	D	D
11	D	D	C	B	C	A & B	B	C	B
12	D	B	D	B	C	C	B	C	A
13	A	B	C	A	A	B	D	A	A
14	B	B	B	A	A	D	D	D	B
15	B	D	B	A & C	B	A	B	C & D	B
16	B & C	B	A	A & D	A	B & C	B	B & D	C
17	B	B	C	A	A & B	D	D	C	A
18	C	D	A	C	B	D	D	D	C
19	A	D	B	A	C	C	A	D	B
20	A	B & D	D	C	C	D	C	C	B
21	D	C	D	A	A	D	D	B & D	D
22	C	A	C & D	A	D	C	A	B	C
23	D	C	A	C	A	C	B	A	D
24	B	C	D	B	B	D	B	A	A

British Citizenship Test Study Guide

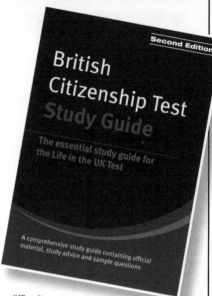

Updated Second Edition

- All the latest official study materials you need to pass the Life in the UK test
- Useful information about the naturalisation application process
- Study advice to help you revise special topics
- Valuable 'Words to know' section that explains difficult terms used in the study materials
- Practice questions and answers to assess your knowledge before sitting the official test
- Discussion and review sections outlining key areas to revise
- Every aspect of the test is explained

Prepare and pass your test first time

Now also with special sections in Hindi, Urdu and Somali

The British Citizenship Test: Study Guide provides revision assistance for anyone wanting to study for the *Life in the UK* citizenship test. Everything you need to prepare for the *Life in the UK Test* is covered in this book, including the official study material from the Home Office and sample questions. This official material has been reproduced from the *Life in the United Kingdom: A Journey to Citizenship* handbook published by the Home Office. *The Life in the UK Test* focuses on content from chapters 2, 3, and 4 of this publication – only these chapters have been reproduced in this study guide. Each section has a set of revision questions so that students can test their understanding of each section.

ISBN 10 : 0-9552159-2-7   ISBN 13 : 978-0-9552159-2-6